EXCAVA ...
BOGHAZ-KEUI
IN THE SUMMER OF 1907

Hugo Winckler and
O. Puchstein

COACHWHIP PUBLICATIONS

Greenville, Ohio

Excavations at Boghaz-Keui in the Summer of 1907,
    by Hugo Winckler and O. Puchstein
© 2013 Coachwhip Publications
Front cover: Namib dunes © Shung-Ho Wang
No claims made on public domain material.
First published in the *Annual Report of the Board of
    Regents of the Smithsonian Institute, 1910*.

ISBN 1-61646-202-7
ISBN-13 978-1-61646-202-4

CoachwhipBooks.com

EXCAVATIONS AT BOGHAZ-KEUI IN THE SUMMER OF 1907.[a]

(With 10 plates.)

By HUGO WINCKLER and O. PUCHSTEIN.

I. THE DISCOVERY OF CLAY TABLETS.

By Hugo Winckler.

Since the beginning of the eighties of the last century, in addition to a deeper study of the ancient civilizations of the countries of the Euphrates and of the Nile, a third region has aroused the interest of investigators. In 1888, A. H. Sayce for the first time collected the inscriptions written in an enigmatic style of hieroglyphics which had become known within a decade and which since then have been coming to light in increasing numbers in north Syria and Asia Minor. It had been contended by William Wright (particularly in his book, The Empire of the Hittites, in 1884) that these inscriptions are connected with the people known as the Cheta or Chatti. This fact is now generally recognized, and adapting the name to its biblical form, Hittim, these people are designated as the "Hittites." Although much careful study has been given to these inscriptions, yet so far there is no definite knowledge as to their meaning.

The interest thus aroused has, however, yielded more tangible results in another direction, and a close examination of records in the Egyptian and Assyrian inscriptions concerning the Cheta or Chatti led to an appreciation of the importance of that people in the history of western Asia. In connection with this research the monuments of Asia Minor were studied, Perrot, in particular, exhibiting a far-seeing view, and it was recognized that the question involved was of a civilization which, in the main, must have embraced all of Asia Minor. The "Hittites" were considered, primarily, as a people of Asia Minor. It became more and more apparent that they entered into the

---

[a] Abstract, translated by permission, from the German, Vorlaüfige Nachrichten über die Ausgrabungen in Bog-haz Köi im Sommer 1907. By Hugo Winckler and O. Puchstein. Mitteilungen der Deutschen Orient-Gesellschaft zu Berlin, No. 35, December, 1907, pp. 1–71.

history of Syria since about the sixteenth century B. C., and the significance of this fact was fully appreciated.

From the Tel el-Amarna letters we learn that a people closely related to the Chatti had at that time pushed its conquests as far as the borders of Babylonia. A recently discovered Babylonian chronicle informs us that the fall of the first Babylonian dynasty, of which Hammurabi was the middle king, was due to an attack of the Chatti. As this attack must have taken place about 1800 B. C., we are thus afforded chronologically definite information of the appearance of this people and their empire.

The accounts in all these documents proved that the center of " Hittite " power had been not in Syria, as was at first believed, but in Asia Minor, though in what part of that country could not be definitely settled. Almost all of the inscriptions in " Hittite " script had come from the region of the Taurus, or southern part of Asia Minor, but this region could not have formed the center of a great empire. The other alternative pointed to Cappadocia which, lying in the very heart of Asia Minor, would be a fit center for a civilized power.

The Tel el-Amarna letters and some clay tablets in cuneiform script found at about the same time as those of Tel el-Amarna in the mound Kul-tepe near the hamlet Kara-eyuk, about three hours east of Kaisariye, bore witness to the strong influence of Babylonian civilization upon the countries of Asia Minor. They showed that the " great King " of Chatti and other rulers of Asia Minor, like those of Syria and Palestine, employed the cuneiform writing in their international dealings.

As early as the thirties of the nineteenth century the ruins of Boghaz-Keui, in the heart of Cappadocia, in the region of the eastern Halys, east of Angora, became known through Texier. They were diligently examined by Perrot and Humann. In the nineties they were visited by E. Chantre, who did some excavating, and by Lieutenant Schaefer and W. Belck, who were all impressed with the importance of these ruins. On my presentation of the matter, Baron W. von Landau offered the means for a trip of inquiry. The required irade was speedily obtained with the aid of the imperial embassy in Constantinople, and thus I reached the ruins in company with Th. Makridy Bey in October, 1905.

The very extent of the ruins indicated that it was a place of unusual importance and that it represented one of the centers of " Hittite " civilization. The prospects of epigraphic acquisitions were very favorable. In the three days during which we could examine the ruins some thirty fragments of clay tablets were discovered, some of them picked up in our presence. In some cases their shape showed that they were parts of tablets of extraordinary size. According to the assertions of the inhabitants of Boghaz-Keui and of other visitors, similar finds had previously been made. During the excavations of the following year (1906) there was a rumor of large bronze finds, consisting of axes and horse trappings. One of these ax-shaped objects is in the Museum of Berlin (fig. 1).

The finds made at our first examination of the ruins promised rich booty of documents in cuneiform script, and through them the establishing on the soil of Asia Minor of a definite historical center that might possibly be connected with other accounts concerning " Hittite " history. The presumptive size of the tablets and the character of the script recalled some of the letters of Tel el-Amarna, so that they could be assumed to be of the same period. Two other facts pointed to a connection between them. All the fragments found at Boghaz-Keui were inscribed in an unknown language, but they were too small to afford connected stories. A chain of circumstances, however,

FIG. 1.—Flat bronze hatchet from Boghaz-keui. ⅔ natural size.

indicated that they were in the same language as two documents of Tel el-Amarna (the letter of Amenophis III to Tarchundaraus, King of Arsawa, and the one in which the prince Lapawa is mentioned), and which goes by the name of the " Arsawa language." This again pointed to an identical period for both sets of documents and a possible closer connection between them. This impression was confirmed by three small pieces, which, by their very appearance and the quality of the clay, strongly recalled the Amarna tablets, but more so by their contents, which were in the Babylonian language, and formed portions of letters to a king.

On the basis of these results the Society of Explorations in Western Asia (Vorderasiatische Gesellschaft) and some of its members provided the means for further excavations. This work was undertaken in the summer of 1906 and resulted in fixing the site and determining its importance and there was discovered a large number of royal documents. For a continuation of the explorations on a larger scale

the German Oriental Society (Deutsche Orient-Gesellschaft) granted
the means, while the German Archeological Institute undertook the
solution of the archeological problems connected with the task. Thus
the work could be taken up, with increased funds, in the summer of
1907. The excavations were carried on as enterprises of the Ottoman
Museum, under the direction of Th. Makridy Bey, to whose singular
ability in dealing with the people much of the success is due.

The excavations were naturally begun at the point where the tablet
fragments had been found, on the slope of Boyuk-Kale (pl. 1). This
is a mountain which had been fortified as a citadel and formed the
northeast corner of the city wall. The work was carried on from
the base upward. The higher the digging ascended the larger was
the size of the tablets found, till in places large tablets were ranged
in layers. There is no question that we have here to do with the
remains of royal archives, though they represent only a small rem-
nant of the original contents.

About midway of the declivity was found the document which established the fact that the site represented the capital of the Chatti
empire. The contents of this document were not new; they were in
Babylonian language and writing, and formed parts of the treaty of
Ramses II with the Cheta King Chetasar, as he has been usually
called, or Hattusil, as now proven by the cuneiform script. The text
had long been known, being inscribed on the walls of the temple of
Karnak.

It was thus ascertained beyond doubt that the tablets belonged to
the royal archives and that consequently the site represented the
capital. But the question still remained, what was the name of this
most important center of the earliest history of Asia Minor, whither
once went the embassies from the courts of Thebes, Babylon, Asshur,
and whence were started undertakings so decisive for the destinies
of the countries of Western Asia? The customary designation of
countries in the new documents is "the country of the city N. N."
The oriental conception underlying this expression is that a " country " is a district which has for its center and seat of the ruler, a
city (machazu) in whose sanctuary the god has his earthly habita-
tion, with the king as his representative and plenipotentiary. A
natural consequence of this view is that country and city bear the
same name. This observation led to the surmise that the name of the
capital was the same as that of the land, Chatti. Subsequently this
was confirmed by documents which told only of the city of Chatti
and its principal divinity, Teshub, who was already known as one
of the most important gods of these and other " Hittite " peoples.

The documents found on the slope of Boyuk-Kale were of the three
Chatti kings who were known from the Ramses treaty, though those
of Hattusil, the last of them, seem to predominate.

PLATE 1.

BOYUK-KALE FROM THE NORTHWEST. *a.* WHERE CLAY TABLETS WERE FOUND. *b.* THE GREAT TEMPLE. TO THE LEFT OF *b,*
HEADQUARTERS OF THE EXPEDITION.

A still larger deposit of tablets was found in the eastern addition of the large building, presumably the principal sanctuary of the God Teshub. Here, too, the documents of Hattusil predominated, and there were pieces pertaining to his two successors, though not an inconsiderable portion belonged to the reign of his two predecessors, particularly Subbiluliuma the first. Other places, besides these two main deposits, yielded considerable finds. Thus one of the gates furnished a large doom book with the royal seal of Arnuanta. (See below.)

The short time that could be devoted during and since the excavations to the investigation of the material has permitted only an examination of those documents which appeared important, especially such as might shed light on historical conditions. A detailed and exhaustive study of the new-found archives must be preceded by the decipherment of the language and will require the cooperation of many workers for a long time. Even the few examples of the contents here given must be taken only as provisional.

But even to convey an adequate idea of what has already been studied is not easy in the present limited space. It will be seen, for instance, that the Tel el-Amarna finds, as well as many data of the Assyrian inscriptions, find their commentary in the new texts. It would be an instructive task to illustrate by comparative examples this unique interlinking of records, but this would require much more space than is here available, and a more thorough investigation of the documents than has been hitherto possible.

The foremost result obtained is the chronological dating of the documents and through this the defining of the city in its constituent parts. There are documents of the reign of seven kings, representing five generations. Four of these kings were already known from the treaty of Ramses, though their names are only now definitely identified. In the uncertain Egyptian script their names were read, Sapalulu, Maurasar, Mautenel, Chetasar. The order as now established is Subbiluliuma, his two sons Arandas and Mursil, followed by his two grandsons, Muttallu and Hattusil, sons of Mursil. The genealogy of the sons of Subbiluliuma begins with him only; his grandson, Hattusil, names the great-grandfather of the same name, not however as the " great king, King of Chatti," but merely as " King of the City Ku-us-sar " (otherwise unknown). He was probably one of the many city kings who appear as vassals of the " great King," while his son Subbiluliuma was the founder of the dynasty. He had a long and successful reign. The Tel el-Amarna finds contain one or two letters of Amenophis III to him. The new documents show that his reign extended at least to that of Amenophis IV. A whole series of events are common to the Amarna letters and the accounts in the Chatti archives. Here is recounted the advance of the Chatti King on Mitani after the death of its king, Tushratta. Founders of dynasties in the Orient are frequently also great conquerors, as in the case of Subbiluliuma. His supremacy is recognized by Azir, ruler of the Amorites, and by other princes of Syria, who in the Amarna letters ask the king of Egypt for protection against him. Mitani, until then an independent state, and under Tushratta victorious over the Chatti, succumbs later, and is completely reduced under his supremacy.

The reign of Arandas, son of Subbiluliuma, seems to have been of short duration. His successor was Arandas's brother Mursil (hitherto read Maurasar). There are quite a number of documents relating to Mursil's reign, but much fewer than of the reign of his father and of his son Hattusil. This would lead to the conclusion that Mursil's reign was shorter than those of either Subbiluliuma or Hattusil, though not absolutely a short one. One document seems to give a survey of the first years of his reign, reaching down to his tenth year. It contains references to the subjection of Mitani by his father and to his own relations with Arsawa, and to a number of territories not hitherto known, such as Gasga, Tibia, Zichria. A still more obscure passage in the document seems to bear on the war with Egypt which resulted in the famous battle of Kadesh.

Mursil's successor was at first his son Muttallu. This is already mentioned in the treaty of Ramses and is dwelt upon by Hattusil in several documents. What his end was is not yet clear. His reign could have lasted but a couple of years. The Amarna documents relate that he deposed one of the Amurri (Amorite) princes and put another in his place. A document of his time contains an enumeration of the Chatti pantheon.

Muttallu was succeeded by his brother Hattusil, who is known through his treaty with Ramses. The larger portion of the archives belongs to his reign, which must have been quite an extended one. The documents give information concerning the most important events of that period. Under him the relations with Amurri were regulated anew. The most important event under Hattusil was the making of a treaty of friendship with Egypt. This is referred to in many letters. The document, which may be considered as the Babylonian text of the treaty, is perhaps merely a preliminary exchange of notes. The negotiations preceding the conclusion of the treaty were carried on, as seen from parts of other letters, with great deliberation, as becoming the dignity of both chanceleries. Even the queens participated in the great event, for Naptera, the wife of Ramses, expressed her joy over it to her " sister," Puduhipa, the spouse of Hattusil, in a special letter.

The relations with the other great powers is illustrated by a letter to the King of Babylon; while a fragment of a letter from the Babylonian King, Katashman-turgu, to Hattusil, shows that the friendly feeling between them was mutual. The constantly growing power of Assyria must have drawn them to one another. The Babylonian King to whom Hattusil's letter is addressed is not named, but must have been Katashman-buriash, son of Katashman-turgu, who is known as an adversary of Shalmaneser I of Assyria. This letter, which comprises upward of 160 long lines, while recalling the Amarna letters, differs from them in its purely political contents. There is no haggling about dowries, or presents promised and not received, as in the long letters between Tushratta and Amenophis III and IV. In Hattusil's letter to the Babylonian King weighty matters of state are discussed, and, especially, information concerning the influence on the succession to the throne exhibits the politics of the great states in their mutual relations:

* * * When thy father died I mourned like a good brother * * * and I sent my messenger and wrote to the notables of Karduniash (Babylonia) as follows: "If you do not recognize [the son] of my brother as King, I shall be your enemy. [But otherwise] if any foe attacks you or is hostile against you, I shall come to your aid." * * * Neither can the people of Chatti command (coerce) those of Karduniash, nor those of Chatti. I wrote to them (the people of Karduniash) with a friendly intent that they may recognize the posterity of my brother Katashman-turgu. * * * As to what my brother writes me that I have stopped diplomatic relations, I did it on account of the Beduin peril (*Ki ah-lamu*—the Aramean Beduins—*Nakru*). * * *

In another passage of the letter Hauttsil informs the Babylonian King about his alliance with the King of Egypt, while still another paragraph treats of a complaint made by the Babylonian King on account of the assassination of trading people (members of a caravan) on their way to Amurri and Ugarit (northern Phenicia, etc.). The writer refutes the possibility of any responsibility resting on the Chatti territory and points out that the murderers should be delivered to the relatives of the murdered.

An insight of wide range into the history of the time is afforded by the following sentences:

I will, furthermore, say to my brother that as regards Banti-shinni, of whom my brother writes, he "disturbs the land." I asked Banti-shinni, and he answered, "I have a claim of 30 talents of silver against the inhabitants of Akkad." But now, since Banti-shinni has become my vassal, my brother may enter a suit against him and he shall answer in the presence of thy ambassador, Adad-shar-ilani, and before the gods [that is, in a formal court action] concerning the disturbances of the country of my brother. And if my brother will not himself prosecute the action, then let thy servant [official] who has heard that Banti-shinni has molested the land of my brother come and carry on the action. Then I shall call Banti-shinni to answer. He is my vassal. In molesting my brother does he not molest myself?

This Banti-shinni is known from other sources, and it will later be seen that he, Prince of Amurri, the Amorite, is one of the successors of Aziri, known or notorious from the Tel el-Amarna letters. Thus the former surmises about the invasions of the different Semitic migrations are raised to certainties. Since the eighth century B. C. the "Arabians," as invading and conquering Bedouins, formed border states between the settled territory and the steppe. Previous to that the "Aramean Bedouins" played the same rôle. A document of the time of the dynasty of Hammurabi relates that "Amurru" were roaming in the steppe, playing the same game. Since at that time the entire Orient, Babylonia included, must have been overrun by a population that was racially related, the conclusion suggested itself that the Semitic stratum was then in a process of " immigration." To it belonged also the Habiri-Hebrews (a substratum of which were the Israelites), of whom there is mention in the Amarna letters. It is now seen that the ruler of the Amorites is not confined to the hinterland of northern Phenicia, as related in the Amarna letters, but that his territory extends to the borders of Babylonia; that is, he is lord over the great Syrian Desert and its borders. He has a claim against the inhabitants of Akkad, a city of North Babylonia. It shows the spread of a people under the name of "Amorite" from Babylonia to northern Palestine. And this development is of the highest importance for the solution of ethnological problems of the Old Testament.

Hattusil's letter then treats of a physician (asu) and an exorciser (ashipu) who had been once sent to Muttallu and had not yet returned. The exchanging of physicians is also referred to in the letters from Egypt. Then the letter again passes into the field of politics and Hattusil gives expression to the paternal benevolence he feels for his young friend and " brother," encouraging him to attack the country of the enemy, by which very likely Assyria is meant, which was the adversary of both.

Hattusil's reign thus exhibits a decline of the Chatti power. The rising power was then Assyria, under Shalmaneser I and Tukulti-Ninib, upon whose death it likewise collapsed.

The reign of the two successors falls in this time. First came Dudhalia, Hattusil's son. One of the larger documents or edicts mentions Puduhipa (his mother) as coregent. As the queen appears in the same rôle under his successor, we have to assume that this was not an exception, but, as elsewhere (for instance, in Aribi, with the Nabateans, the Ptolemies), that it was the rule. The queen shares in the power of government by her own right, not as wife of the reigning king, for it is the mother who is named in close relation to her son. So, also, as regards Egypt, Tushratta, in a letter to Amenophis IV, appeals to Queen Teyi, and in one of the Tel el-Amarna letters the Babylonian King Burnaburiash complains that this same queen has not shown sufficient interest in his fate. The letter of Naptera to Puduhipa, mentioned above, in which she expresses her satisfaction over the concluded alliance, would show that queens acted independently even in the lifetime of their husbands.

The edict of Dudhalia seems to bear on the regulation of internal affairs concerning the possessions of powerful subjects, and enumerates many cities and places, closing with the names of witnesses.

A treaty (in private possession) with the King of Aleppo (Halab) containing, like other similar documents, an historical introduction seems likewise to have been drawn up during his reign.

Dudhalia's son and successor, Arnuanta, is at present known only from three documents—two fragments of edicts and the doom book found in the gate of the inner wall. The latter bears the royal seal with a Hittite and cuneiform legend. The former is broken off; the latter may be read:

[Se]al of the edict (tabarna) of Arnuanta, great King, son of Du-u[d-ha-li.
[S]eal of lady Ta-wa-ash-shi (??), lady Mu-ni-Dan, great Queen, * * *?, daughter of Du-ud-ha-li-i[a].

Was the first of the two ladies named the mother—that is, the wife of Dudhalia? His own wife was also his sister—another instance of marriage between brother and sister in the royal house—which here, as among the Pharohs, may have had a mythological reason. The Chatti King, too, was the " sun "—like the Pharaoh or Inca.

There seem to be no other accounts of this reign. The reign of Arnuanta in all probability coincided with the great retrogression of Assyria after the fall of Tukulti-Ninib. As Egypt was likewise weak at that time, it is to be assumed that the territory of the Hittite peoples was not much exposed to its influence from about 1250 to 1150 B. C., and as a consequence we have no records for that period. It is only under Tiglath-Pileser I that we have further accounts, from which fact it may be concluded that the Chatti land also has passed through great revolutions which led to the decay of the state. Tiglath-Pileser defeated the Chatti King and was thereupon recognized by Egypt as the legitimate successor to the Chatti claims in Syria and northern Palestine. Henceforth " Chatti land " is for Assyria a territory standing under Assyrian supremacy, but the term is also limited to Syria and northern Palestine. In Asia Minor there are now for Assyria only " Muski," who appear in place of the former Chatti state.

Alongside of Chatti, the state of Mitani seems, according to the Amarna letters, to have played the most important part. The numerous and lengthy letters of King Tushratta and the similar relations to Egypt entertained by his two predecessors warranted this conclusion. It seemed strange that this correspondence broke off immediately after the accession of Amenophis IV.

It was possible to infer from other documents that the territory of Mitani had fallen to rising Assyria, which shortly before was its inferior in power, since Tushratta has been in possession even of Nineveh. From other documents it can be seen that a people such as are shown to have been in Mitani was spread as far as the borders of Babylonia and since, according to the Amarna letters, the same fact may be assumed for Palestine, it may be concluded that previous to the Amarna period a people to whom the name of "Mitani" was applied had carried on a large migration or conquest.

The treaties between Subbiluliuma and the successor of Tushratta partly confirm these conclusions and partly put them in a new light. In particular a new light is shed on the question of the composition of the population of Mesopotamia and Syria.

In the first place the political conditions are fully explained through the treaties. Their historical introductions contain accounts of the development of affairs and, in a measure, give a survey of the history of the state of Mitani. The cessation of information concerning Tushratta in Tel el-Amarna becomes clear; he must soon have found his end of which the treaty speaks. That there should be no correspondence between the successors of Tushratta and the Egyptian King is understood when one reads in the treaties that Mitani after a period of anarchy came under the supremacy of Chatti and therefore could not hold direct diplomatic relations with the Egyptian court. Thus these data form a commentary to those letters of Tel el-Amarna which bear on the affairs of Mitani and Chatti, that is, north Syria. The same countries and the same persons are met with in them, and we see how the individual princes are drawn hither and thither between the great powers, shaping their conduct according to the condition of affairs.

The narrative part of the treaty relates how Tushratta, the King of Mitani, rose against the King of Chatti, whereupon the latter inflicted depredations on the left bank of the Euphrates (the territory of Tushratta) and annexed the mountain range of Niblani. But Tushratta was defiant and threatened to retaliate by plundering the right bank of the Euphrates (the territory of Chatti). The record then goes on to say:

The great King (of Chatti) defied him. For at the time of the father of the King of Chatti (that is Hattusil I) the country of Isuwa rebelled. People of Chatti went to Isuwa (because) the people of the city * * * had rebelled at the time of my father. But the sun (designation of the King of Chatti) Subbiluliuma defeated them. At that time the people who escaped my hand went to Isuwa * * *.

But the sun Subbiluliuma undertook an expedition against the defiant king Tushratta. I crossed the Euphrates. I marched against Isuwa and visited punishment upon the entire Isuwa. I made them a second time my subjects. I inflicted punishment upon all the people and lands that at the time of my father went to Isuwa * * * and subjected them to Chatti. The lands which I captured I released, they remained in their place. But the people whom I released migrated to their people and the Chatti took possession of their country.

The occurrence which is here alluded to illustrates peculiar conditions in the old Orient. An entire people migrates, seeking new habitations in a land of foreign lords. There was no lordless land in the old Orient, although the more frequently these lands were really unprotected by the lords. A similar movement (in which Isuwa is also mentioned) is recorded in a treaty which regulated the relation of the Chatti King Mursil or Hattusil (probably the first) to Sunassura of Kizwadna. This country, too, seceded at the time of the " grandfather " (of the Chatti King) to the Charri, and this was accomplished by migrations to Isuwa. The biblical migrations of Abraham's people to Palestine and Egypt and of the Israelites from Egypt appear in a new light, just as here a discontented people seeks a home in a defenseless or poorly protected land of another lord, whose rule is less oppressive and allows of freer development, so did the Israelites migrate to another land.

The historical introduction of the treaty describes other expeditions and conquests of the Chatti King which were provoked by the hostility of Tushratta and mentions other countries and persons who are in part met with in the Amarna and Assyrian inscriptions. The document then reviews the reason for the present treaty, at the same time giving an account of the end of Mitani:

When his son and his servants had entered a conspiracy and killed his father, Tushratta, * * * Teshub decided the case in favor of Arbatama, and the land of Mitani was entirely ruined. The Assyrians and Alsheians divided it. But the great King [of Chatti] until then did not cross the Euphrates nor exact taxes and tribute from the country of Mitani. When he learned of the poverty of Mitani he sent them palace people [that is, members of the royal house], cattle, sheep, and horses, for the Charri people got there into misery. Suttatava, together with the notables, sought to kill Mattiuaza, the son of the King. He fled and came to the sun Subbiluliuma. The great King said: " His case was decided by Teshub, taking the hand [helping] of Mattiuaza, son of King Tushratta, I place him upon the throne. * * * " The great King gave the country of Mitani, for the sake of his daughter, a new life. I took Mattiuaza by the hand and gave him my daughter for a wife.

Here ends the introduction to the treaty. There then follow the conditions regulating the relation of Mattiuaza to his protector. He enters into a " sonship." His empire is thus not properly a vassalage, but something like a protectorate. He is to dismiss all his wives and have only the daughter of the Chatti King as wife. Their offspring shall be heirs to the throne. Between Chatti and Mitani shall be friendship. Regulations regarding the extradition of " fugitives," similar to those of the treaty with Egypt, are agreed upon. At the conclusion the gods of both countries are invoked as witnesses of the alliance.

The account of the events after Tushratta's death opens new vistas into the conditions of the various countries. The Charri must have played a part in Mitani, which accounts for the mentioning of their King Artatama at the beginning of the treaty. They may represent a people living under their own King toward Asia Minor, but who overran Mitani and seized the reins of government.

There are scarcely any documents bearing directly upon Assyria, though a fragment speaks of "Adad-nirai, your lord," which may be part of a letter from Subbiluliuma to that Assyrian King.

From the data known before the present excavations were undertaken it was expected that instead of the center of the Chatti Empire, the country of Arsawa (Arsapi) would be mentioned. It was not surprising, therefore, to find this country often referred to in the new documents, and while it seems to have always been under the influence of the King of Chatti, it must have been an independent state, for Amenophis III writes directly to its King, Tarchundaraus, and a diplomatic intercourse could be maintained only with independent states. The country must have been situated somewhere within Asia Minor. Fragments of a lengthy tablet (in the Hittite language) record the affairs of Arsawa. There is mention of King Alakshandu, evidently a contemporary of Hattusil (and probably also of Mursil, who is likewise mentioned), and who was at all events a successor of Tarchundaraus, as the latter must have been a contemporary of Subbiluliuma.

Less frequent is the occurrence of Alashia-Cyprus, which in the Tel el-Amarna finds is represented by its own letters. In the fragment in which it is mentioned it is referred to, as in the Amarna letters, as furnishing copper, its main product.

Aitakuma, Prince of Kinza, known from the Amarna letters, is met with in the historical portion of the Mattiuaza treaty and elsewhere. His son, Shama-Teshub, is represented by his own letters.

Most remarkable is the overlapping of both archives (of Tel el-Amarna and Chatti) in their accounts concerning the country of Amurri and its princes. The importance inherent in the "Amorites" as old settlers of Palestine and Phenicia is now augmented when it can be seen how everything developed from the conditions of a great immigration, and what attitude the Amorite people of Canaan and Phenicia assumed toward the other peoples of this immigration, including the Habiri.

In the Amarna letters Aziri, Prince of Amurri, plays in northern Phenicia the part of a disturber of the peace. Aside from several of his own letters to the Egyptian court, he is very frequently mentioned in the letters of the other princes as the soul of all disturbances. The capture and destruction by him of the city of Sumur in the territory of Byblos forms the subject of many complaints and much correspondence. The court of Egypt ordered him to rebuild (though not to vacate) the city, and finally summoned him to appear at court and defend himself. After many subterfuges and delays he went to Egypt and succeeded in exonerating himself. But the accusations of his opponents that he was in sympathy with Chatti were as little unfounded as in the case of the Prince of Kinza. Subbiluliuma and his successors themselves state that Aziri at last became a faithful vassal of Chatti and so also remained his successors. The conditions of his country are touched upon in several royal edicts and treaties—composed in Hittite and Assyrian—so that we obtain a kind of chronicle of Amurri from the time of Subbiluliuma and Aziri down to that of their great-grandchildren. Thus Mursil, addressing Abi-Teshub, the grandson of Aziri, says:

> Aziri, thy grandfather, rebelled against my father. My father reduced him to submission. When the kings of Nuhashi and Kinza rose against my father, thy grandfather Aziri did not rise. When * * * my father made war upon his enemies, thy grandfather Aziri likewise made war on them * * * And my father gave protection to Aziri and his land * * * 300 (shekel) of gold my father imposed upon thy grandfather as a present and tribute. He paid them annually, never withheld them, never angered him * * * As thy grandfather Aziri behaved toward my father, so he behaved toward me. When the kings of Nuhashi and Kinza again rose against me, thy grandfather Aziri and thy father Du-Teshub did not join them.

In a document, written in the Hittite language, belonging to the time of Dudhalia, the name of one of the Amurri Kings, Benteshina, is the equivalent of the Assyrian Put-ahi, from *putu*, front, and *ahu*, brother. The name Benteshina is not " Hittite " in the narrower sense (Chatti), but belongs to the other of the two known languages—the one which until now was designated as " Mitani." It is therefore certain that the Amurri princes at that time bore names in this language.

From this fact may be derived conclusions of great significance for the ethnology of the countries here discussed. Until now the Semitic constituents of the Syrian population, sufficiently known, were considered as the only or predominating factors in western Asia. The new information compels us to give also the other element, the " Hittite," its due importance, and allows us to distinguish new components in that general and indefinite ethnic name.

The designation " Mitani " has been a provisional one. It can be now established that the propagation of that language, and also of the people, extended from the borders of Babylonia to Egypt. This propagation must have been old. According to a Babylonian chronicle a great conquest by a people bearing the name of Chatti took place at the end of the first Babylonian dynasty; that is, soon after 2000 B. C., or, at the latest, at 1700 B. C. From this time on the name Chatti must be connected with the populations that overran western Asia. It is obvious that this " Hittite " population could not have remained for a millenium and more as a single united people. The question is, What is the relation of our Chatti of Subbiluliuma's dynasty and their language to those conquerors?

In the first place, it is clear that we have here to do with two different languages, as different as Latin and Greek. The " Mitani " tongue must be considered as the earlier one in western Asia; it is the language of the older strata of the migration. The question is only, Was it the language of the " Chatti " conquerors at the end of the first Babylonian dynasty, or did these Chatti already speak the " Hittite " language? This question can not here be definitely decided. For the present it may be stated that in the Assyrian inscriptions Mitani is considered as the language of Mesopotamia, and as thus having a sure footing within the narrower sphere of Babylonian civilization, while the Tel el-Amarna documents attest to its use also in Palestine. Taking this evidence in connection with the new information it may now be stated as a certainty that before the Tel el-Amarna period a people, such as may be comprised under the name of " Hittite," and which was identical with the one until now best known by the name of " Mitani," spread as far as the southern borders of Palestine.

From this conclusion it follows that we have to count with a very considerable non-Semitic layer in the population of Syria over which the Israelitish or " Hebrew " layer was later superimposed. The differentiation of the component parts of this " Hittite " layer can only be undertaken after a more thorough investigation of the language of Mitani and the " Hittite."

In the accounts of conditions after Tushratta's death the Charri play a part. There is no question that they were a population of Mitani, forming the ruling or aristocratic class. By the side of this there is also a people of Charri, evidently closely related to that of Mitani, having its own kings, thus forming a state by itself. The simple explanation would be that a great Charri conquest took place, which concerned Mesopotamia and the adjacent countries. From their royal family Tushratta became king of Mitani, thus attempting to support his power by the part of the population that was older than the Charri (but likewise " Hittite "). That would have been the usual course of things under such conditions.

As to the situation of the state of Charri, it must be placed in the immediate neighborhood of Mitani, in Mesopotamia, rather northward than southward—that is, in the direction of Armenia. But here we recall that the Egyptian accounts also mention a country of Cha-ru, and both names can not well be separated. In these records, however, Cha-ru was taken as the designation of southern Palestine, which would carry the name a long distance away. This difficulty is

removed by our assumption of an extensive immigration and conquest. The designation of southern Palestine as "Charu" in the
Egyptian accounts would only show that just then (in the time of
Sety I), or shortly before, the Charu conquest took place, which extended the name Charu to the southern borders.

But a difficulty arises when a detailed separation of the several
strata of the population is attempted. In the first place there are
the two languages—the "Mitani" and the new "Hittite." They do
not seem to be related, but whether they belong to different families
of languages must for the present remain undecided. The "Hittite,"
the former "Arsawa," has been claimed for the Indo-European family
of languages (compare Knudzon, Die Zwei Arsawa Briefe). It is
rather premature, however, to pass judgment on this question before
the new documents have been subjected to a closer study. There can
be no longer any doubt that we should assume the existence here of
an Indo-European population. As guardians of the treaties between
Chatti and Mitani (Mattiuaza) the gods of both countries are invoked. These are, in the first place, the divinities established of old,
that go back to the earlier periods of purely Babylonian influence,
for they bear pure Babylonian names. Then comes the Teshub-circle,
evidently the properly constituted national deities of both countries
but likewise belonging to an older stratum. In the midst of these
names we suddenly find, in the Mitani portion, two names hardly to be
expected in this connection:

1. ilâni-mi-it-ra-ash-shi-il u-ru-w-na-ash-shi-el (variant: a-ru-na-ash-shi-il).
2. ilu (!) in-dar ilâni na-asha-a[t-ti-ia-a]n-na (variant: in-da-ra na-
    sh[a]-at-ti-ia-an-na).

That is, Mithra, Varuna—whose identity can not be doubted,
though the rendering of his name offers some difficulty—Indra, and
a fourth divinity, who from the context must belong to the same
group.

It is impossible here to enlarge upon the significance of this fact
as evidence of the existence of an Indo-European people in western
Asia. Suffice it here to answer briefly the question: To which part
of the population do these divinities belong? The god of Mitani, as
also of Chatti, is Teshub; he would thus represent the older layer.
The layer represented by the Indo-European divinities must have
been the dominant and aristocratic one, since its gods are invoked by
name. This points to the Charri, who must therefore have been
Aryans.

Since our Hittite language is Indo-European, we shall further
assume that the same population also overran the Chatti land, so that
for Chatti, as well as for Mesopotamia and Syria-Palestine, two strata
must be assumed, the earlier Teshub-people and the younger Charri.
With this assumption accords the use of the Hittite language in Palestine and the character of proper names, such as Mattiuaza, or that

of a Syrian prince, Namiawaza. On the other hand, none of the names of the royal family of Mitani and Charri is formed with that of the principal god Teshub, while that of the oldest member is Saush-shatar, the second part of which corresponds to Aryan Kshatra, as rendered in cuneiform script. The same observation is made with regard to the members of the royal family of Chatti.

Considering the ethnology of earliest Palestine, it hardly need be pointed out that the Charri are the Horim of the Old Testament.

The two strata of people, represented by their languages, may be designated as the Aryan and the Teshub. There are indications that the Teshub-strata was superimposed upon a still older one. The chief god of Chatti, as well as of Mitani, was Teshub, the national sanctuary at the city of Chatti being consecrated to him. But other divinities are recorded, bearing in part purely Babylonian names (as Zagaga), who must belong to the earlier periods of Babylonian influence. A predominating part is also played by the cult of the sun. The " sun of (the city of) Arinna " is frequently mentioned, and seems to rival with Teshub for the supremacy, so that it must have been a famous sanctuary of high antiquity.

Compared with the rich harvest of written documents, the finds of sculptures were not large. The immense area of the temple, the principal building, yielded nothing of the kind. It must have been previously ransacked. Only in the court of the temple were there found remnants of a water basin. One piece of the basin lay on the surface and was formerly considered as the " throne; " it is as such described by Perrot and Chipiez. One end is formed by two lions with their fore parts turned outward. The other end is represented by a corresponding figure of a lion, only of a considerably larger size. Their relation is that of a full-grown animal to a young one (pl. 2, figs. 1 and 2). Aside from this the city gates furnished some of the best examples of Hittite art. A specimen is here reproduced, the lion's gate (from a drawing of O. Puchstein, pl. 3). The finds at other gates brought to light by the excavations of the Archeological Institute are better reserved for discussion by specialists.

These objects will probably have to be placed in the same period as the documents. To an earlier stage of art belong two stone blocks found on the mountain declivity above the " temple " (pls. 4 and 5). They apparently served as bases of statues. Though the general meaning of the representation is evidently a symbolical scene, yet the interpretation of the individual objects will present many riddles. No indications of the former placement of the two pieces could be found. Further search resulted only in finding the head of a clay statuette of the Hellenistic period. There was a rich harvest of potteries. All the different epochs from the Hittite to the Galatian periods are probably represented by numerous samples. The treatment of this subject must likewise be left to specialists.

FIG. 1.—TWO SMALLER LIONS OF THE WATER BASIN.

FIG. 2.—LARGER LION OF THE WATER BASIN.

PLATE 3.

VIEW OF THE OUTER SOUTH GATE, WITH LIONS, AND OF THE LEFT TOWER.

Hittite Relief Discovered Above the Temple.

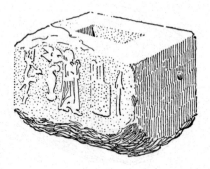

HITTITE RELIEF DISCOVERED ABOVE THE TEMPLE.

II. The Buildings of Boghaz-Keui.

By O. Puchstein.

That the Imperial Archeological Institute was enabled to undertake the solution of the archeological tasks connected with Prof. H. Winckler's new explorations in 1907 was due to the kindness of Dr. O. Hamdy Bey, director-general of the Imperial Ottoman Museum, and was made possible by the special grant of His Majesty, the German Emperor. Some of the expenses were defrayed by Professor Winckler from funds placed at his disposal.

While Makridy Bey, of the Ottoman Museum, had started the new excavations in April, the government archeologist, Daniel Krencker, and Dr. Ludwig Curtius, who were at first commissioned by the central direction of the institute, could not set out before the end of May and begin their work before the first of June. Doctor Curtius remained on the scene till the end of August. After the end of June Krencker was assisted by the government architect, Heinrich Kohl, and after his departure, in the middle of July, was superseded by him. From the middle of July the secretary-general of the institute was digging and working alongside of Kohl, both carrying on the excavations tentatively begun by Makridy Bey and Winckler in 1906.

It was a great advantage for our archeological investigations that Winckler's discoveries had determined the period and the sphere of civilization to which the finds of Boghaz-Keui belonged. On this sure basis Doctor Curtius studied the well-known rock reliefs and examined the new sculpture finds. He gained much new material for defining the authentic Hittite monochrome ceramics and the multiform " Phrygian," faintly tinted potsherds, so that the question as to whether the latter belonged, in part at least, to the Hittite period of Boghaz-Keui can now be settled.

The additions to the knowledge of Hittite architecture in Cappadocia made by the work of the institute is of much scientific importance. The buildings were large and monumental, and acquaint us with a new style of oriental architecture.

Considering first, from an archeological viewpoint, the buildings, there may be recalled the data given by Winckler about Boyuk-Kale, the main acropolis of Chatti, where the first more recent archives were found. We ourselves did not work on this site of the city district, but the examination of the remains which Makridy Bey brought to light (" a " on pl. 1) were of great assistance for the knowledge of the general character of Hittite architecture. What we saw was the eastern half of several small rooms located on the edge of the large plateau of the Boyuk-Kale and supported by fortress walls (pl. 6). While the foundation of the walls of the rooms consists of quarry stones, bound with loam, the walls themselves, about 1 meter thick, were once constructed of strong wooden joists or panels, with sundried bricks in single files. When fire destroyed the building, the woodwork vanished, its space being filled with débris and rubble (" b " on pl. 6), while the brickwork was burnt red, so that the walls are still about 1 meter above the ground (" a " on pl. 6). In one of these rooms, shoved into those parts of the wall from which the woodwork was burnt out, cuneiform tablets of the archives are said to have been found. The latter may have been originally preserved either in the basement or in the upper story.

The nature of the building to which the archive rooms belonged, whether palace or temple, can not be determined until further excavating is done. It extends far eastward over the plateau of the acropolis and has left remnants on the surface as well as under ground.

More definite details can be obtained about the site of the second archive which Makridy Bey discovered in the spring of 1907 before our arrival. A detailed account of the circumstances under which the cuneiform tablets were discovered and a discussion of the question as to how they came to this place is discussed by Winckler. In our opinion the archive remains were lying at the east side of the large building which has been taken for a palace. After a thorough examination by Krencker it was shown to have been a colossal temple. It was surrounded on all sides by paved streets, and close by, as at the Egyptian temples and old Cretan palaces, stood the vaults or magazines, narrow structures in regular arrangement, which, though once destroyed by fire, still contain the complete number, though in broken condition, of the vessels for receiving the revenues in kind of the temple. In some of the rooms of the eastern magazine (" b " on pl. 7) the tablets were found between the foundation walls. The mode of building the magazines was the same as that of the archives on the Boyuk-Kale, walls of panel work and sun-dried bricks upon stone foundations, only that here the walls entirely disappeared.

The temple itself was built in the same or a similar manner, only more solidly; the thick walls had a socle, about a meter high, of large blocks above the foundation. Hence after the destruction of the upper part by fire, enough remained of the stone socle to determine the ground plan of the entire building. This exhibits in general the character of the Mediterranean temple, but is substantially different from the temple plans of Mesopotamia, Egypt, and North Syria. It represents a quadrangular court; on the south it is accessible by a peculiar portal, and on the north side is a pillared hall; behind, in the midst of a group of rooms, there is a space, peculiar by its situation and its windows, which reach down to the socle, and in it, at the north wall, there is a large pedestal (" a " to

PLATE 6.

ROOMS ON THE BOYUK-KALE IN WHICH THE FIRST EARLIER CLAY TABLET ARCHIVES WERE DISCOVERED.

PLATE 7.

VIEW OF THE GREAT TEMPLE (*a*) FROM THE SOUTHEAST, AND OF THE EAST MAGAZINE (*b*).

PLATE 8.

ADYTUM, OR SACRED CHAMBER, OF THE GREAT TEMPLE. *a.* PEDESTAL FOR THE IDOL. *b–e.* WINDOW SILLS. *f.* THRESHOLD OF PORTAL TO NEXT ROOM.

PLATE 9.

JENIDSCHE-KALE CITADEL IN THE CENTER OF BOGHAZ-KEUI.

" e " on pl. 8), doubtless for the statue of the god who was here venerated. Winckler surmises that it was the god Teshub who once dwelt in this principal temple of Chatti.

The general arrangement of the temple was typical. Kohl proved the existence of, and then excavated, three other buildings of the same kind in the ancient city area—in the upper city. They are located, like the large one, upon natural terraces. A fifth building, close to the structure at the east gate, where in 1906 some tentative digging was done, exhibits an entirely different plan. It seems to have been a palace. The latter, like the four temples, exhibits peculiar elements within the type of old oriental architecture and is specifically North Hittite. We have thus gained a clear conception of the manner of building characteristic of the interior of Asia Minor in the second millenium B. C.

The importance of the site of the city has been pointed out by Winckler. The area, inclosed by fortress walls, is situated on the declivity of a mountain and at its foot. Its view is grander and more impressive than would appear from Humann's excellent chart of 1882, by reason of its wide expanse, its terrace-shaped construction, the great difference in height between the more level lower city and the more rolling upper city, and, finally, on account of the projecting summits and rocks, some of which were specially adapted for citadels. The city must have once presented a view similar to the Syrian fortress in Egyptian pictures. Kohl, with the surveying board, has made a new, careful, and accurate plan of Boghaz-Keui (pl. 9).

The general plan of the city, as well as the walls with their towers and gates, which no doubt belong to the same period as the temples and the palace, are on a grander scale than was to be expected from former accounts. The part of the walls constructed of large stones recalls in its technique the fortifications of the citadels of Mycenæ, which belong to about the same period, though not exactly identical with it. The principal wall of Boghaz-Keui stood upon a mighty earthern rampart, whose slope was plastered with stones. A similar construction is observed in Senjirli, North Syria. The wall averaged 5 meters in thickness, in places 8 meters, and consisted of a high stone socle or basement, of which some remnants remain; and upon this rose, according to authentic vestiges, a structure of wood and sun-dried bricks. The towers projected beyond the wall and were mostly in close proximity to one another.

In front of this principal wall, upon the slope of the rampart, stood another weaker wall, likewise provided with towers. Such a double wall also protected Senjirli, in North Syria, though it was constructed after another scheme, and similar fortifications are now brought to light in Babylon and Asshur.

The so-called sally ports of Boghaz-Keui were very strong. They were narrow but high passages, vaulted with corbel, which led at some places through the rampart and were in parts 72 meters long. They were probably constructed for purposes of defense and served as sally gates.

The part of the wall most exposed to attack, in the south of the city, was more closely examined. The tower that stood in the center, on the highest point of the wall, was built as a gate tower whose entrance, both within and without, was flanked with sphinxes; fragments of the best preserved of these are now in Constantinople. At both ends of the front wall of attack, steep stone steps led from the ground through the plaster of the slope of the high wall to the end tower of the front wall.

Finally, as regards the city gates, we completed the uncovering of the south and east gates, which was begun by Makridy Bey in 1906, and excavated the two west gates, which were close together. At the lower west gate was found the tablet of Arnuanta mentioned above. Each of the towers was flanked by a gate. The plan of the gates is very simple, including a chamber about the same width as the wall, which could be closed on either side. The framings of the openings consisted of large stones, constructed on the same principle as the roofing of the sally ports of a high elliptical corbel vault, but below it had colossal posts surmounted by two or three stones which gradually projected and inclosed the elliptical curve. While at the south gate (pl. 3) both posts are decorated with large lions on the outside, at the east gate (pl. 10) only the inside of the left post bears a sculpture, probably representing a young warrior in life size, who, like an Egyptian king, is clad only with apron and helmet, standing in the usual posture—the left hand balled, while in the right he holds a magnificent battle-ax. Unfortunately, there is no inscription attached to the figure, though it doubtless represents a Hittite king, either Subbiluliuma or Hattusil, or some other one who might have erected the walls and gates of Chatti. This royal figure and the lions at the east gate are, from an art standpoint, the finest and most important sculptures of the old Hittites so far known. European museums should at least procure plaster casts of them.

PLATE 10.

EAST GATE, FROM WITHIN.

Coachwhip Publications

CoachwhipBooks.com

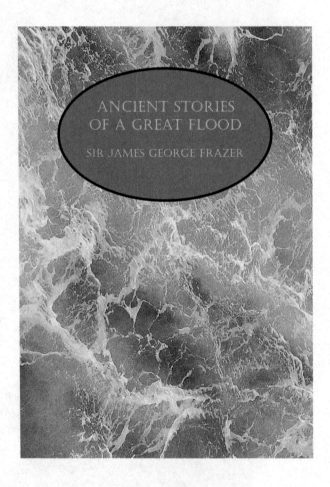

Ancient Stories of a Great Flood
ISBN 1616461713

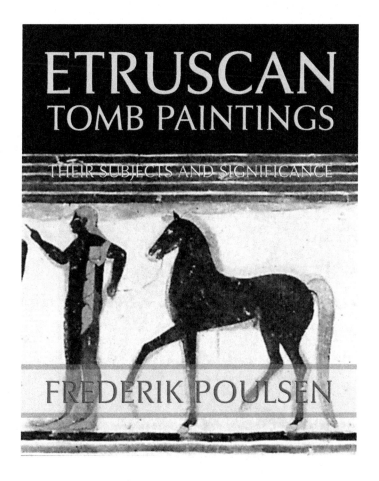

Etruscan Tomb Paintings
ISBN 1616461217

COACHWHIP PUBLICATIONS

COACHWHIPBOOKS.COM

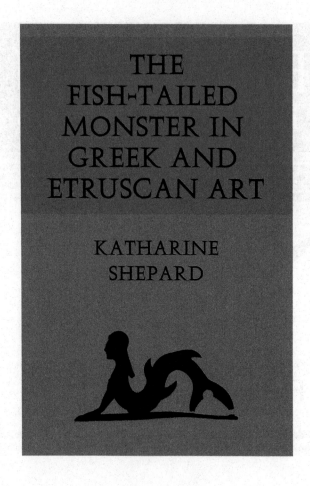

THE
FISH-TAILED
MONSTER IN
GREEK AND
ETRUSCAN ART

KATHARINE
SHEPARD

The Fish-Tailed Monster in Greek and Etruscan Art
ISBN 1616460741

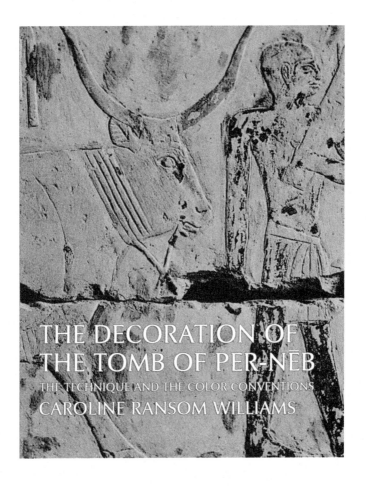

The Decoration of the Tomb of Per-neb
ISBN 1616461225

CPSIA information can be obtained
at www.ICGtesting.com
Printed in the USA
LVOW02s1024170916
4162LVUK00002B/3/P

9 781616 462024